Barbara D Livingston

FOUR SEASONS
Of Racing

A YEAR IN PHOTOGRAPHS

FOUR SEASONS
Of Racing

BARBARA D. LIVINGSTON

THE BLOOD-HORSE, INC.
LEXINGTON, KENTUCKY

ISBN 1-58150-012-2

Printed in Hong Kong by Everbest Printing Company
through Four Colour Imports Ltd., Louisville, KY

First Edition: August 1998

1 2 3 4 5 6 7 8 9 10

C O N T E N T S

 13 SPRING

SUMMER  47

 81 AUTUMN

WINTER  111

Preface 8

Acknowledgments 10

Introduction 11

About the Photographer 142

To my best friend Michael Perry Tyner,

with whom I shared some eighty seasons

PREFACE

By Barbara D. Livingston

T. V. Commercial, Corn Off the Cob, My Dad George — my first memories of horse racing are of watching Kentucky Derbys with my father, and being fascinated by the interesting names of the horses. By the age of eleven, I eagerly awaited section five of the New York *Times* every Sunday, clipping the horse racing photographs and articles. Such articles were plentiful back then, as an incredible chestnut colt by Bold Ruler was busy etching his name into the history books. I was fortunate to be young at a time when, according to that year's New York *Times* year end edition, "In 1973, the Sports Hero was a Horse."

On a rainy morning in August of that year, my mother took me to Saratoga to see that colt, with Ronnie Turcotte up, splash through a sloppy 7 a.m. workout. Some 5,000 people watched Secretariat shatter track records for several distances that morning — although it wasn't official — while under wraps. Just a week later, I still marveled at his majesty, even in defeat, as he was passed by Onion in the Whitney Handicap. I was hooked.

My family probably did not understand my addiction to this sport, and my grandmother eyed me disapprovingly when I handed her drawings I had proudly made of Man o' War "at stud." But it was a true addiction, and I spent countless hours drawing such magic horses as Az Igazi, Raise a Cup, and T. V. Commercial, often creating their features from my imagination.

Hours were also spent studying the work of early equine photographers — the great names of the past such as C. C. Cook, Skeets Meadors, and Bert Clark Thayer. Their photographs were a thing of wonder to me.

They put a white-rimmed-eyed face to the name Gallant Fox, showed me Assault's club foot, recorded the incredible majesty of Man o' War throughout his career. There were no photographs more magic than those of the original Big Red, back swayed, head incredibly high, and eyes glowing with pride, belying his advanced age of thirty.

The new Big Red provided me with my first chance to record racing, which I did both dutifully and pitifully. Saratoga became a grand backdrop for me, and the wonder of those mornings is captured forever, however amateurish, in images of such stars as Forego, Seattle Slew, Ruffian, and Affirmed and Alydar. Lacking the talent to be an equine painter like my idol Richard Stone Reeves, I just knew that I would be a racing photographer.

Meanwhile, I absorbed every Thoroughbred photograph I could find — the discovery of stallion and farm brochures being a new wealth of imagery. I pored over photos of Raja Baba at Hermitage Farm, Dr. Fager at Tartan Farms, and I could finally put a solid face to T. V. Commercial with the aid of a Windfields brochure — a chestnut with a blaze rather than a black and white 13-inch TV image. Acquiring my first issue of *The Blood-Horse* in August of 1974 secured my fate — I had to be published in that magazine, a publication which that very week featured a photographic essay on Saratoga.

My first cover for *The Blood-Horse* came in 1986, and I have been very fortunate since. Mornings at Saratoga have never lost their magic for me, nor farm visits, nor

Breeders' Cup trips, nor the two years I spent following Cigar. Hialeah, which is the most beautiful track I have ever seen, is still a world of movie stars, Citation, and War Admiral in my eyes. And the racehorses of today, from the heart of Dixie Brass, the sheer beauty of Flag Down, the speed of Lite the Fuse, and the wonder of every Alydar offspring, are a constant inspiration for me to try to capture on film.

As I sometimes tell my family, "I am famous — it's just that nobody knows me." That is fine, as I want my photographs to be remembered, rather than my name. In the future, I want young girls to see historical photographs of Cigar and marvel at his white-rimmed eye, or at the wiseness which is so deeply etched in Prairie Bayou's kind face.

In the autumn of 1996, I visited Northview Stallion Station in Maryland to photograph their stallions. As this beautiful farm was once Windfields, it was an easy place to work, and their stallion roster was equally impressive. Among them were such fine animals as Two Punch, Concern, Opening Verse, and Smarten, and they brought each one in to clean up for the photo session.

While waiting, I noticed one gentleman leading up an old timer who was not included in our shoot, a chestnut horse with his head low and his step slowed with time. His coat was dulled with the years of the elements, but his face markings were vaguely familiar to me. "Him? That's old T. V. Commercial," a groom answered my inquiry, waving toward the pair.

I could not believe he was still alive — the first name I remember, from almost thirty years before. Time was short that day, with a full roster to shoot, and the light shifted quickly. But we couldn't resist. They quickly rubbed T. V.'s face clean, brought him to our chosen spot, and stood him for a portrait. Most

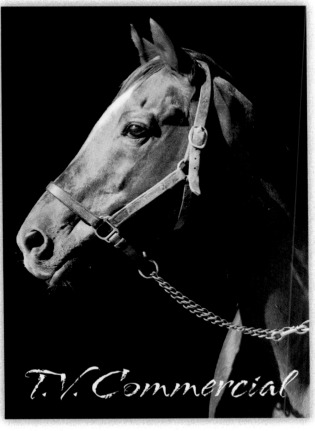

T. V. Commercial

horses require special noises or tricks to entice them to put their ears forward, but not this old boy. He immediately struck a pose of immense pride. Long since pensioned, he glowed with dignity and, while his muddy halter obscured his name plate, it could not hide the nobility in his eyes.

After the day's shoot, I visited with T. V. Commercial. I found a brush, and slipped into his stall. He stood silently, enjoying his visitor, and I brushed his body slowly, sweeping the soft brush over his flanks, down his long neck, along the swayed back.

Before leaving, I stopped at his head. His ears flicked with interest and, with the limits that accompany three decades, he nipped at me. I easily averted his teeth, and, amused, extended my shirt tail. He reached out again, this time his teeth clamping firmly on the material. He stood satisfied, victorious, watching me as I feigned a tugging match.

I eventually slipped my finger into the corner of his mouth, and he dropped the shirt. He had won. I left his stall, said goodbye to him, and clasped the bolt shut behind me.

A few weeks later, at the very advanced age of 31, T. V. Commercial quietly passed away. As I sat in my car reading the small entry in *The Blood-Horse*'s stud news, I wept for my new — and yet oldest — equine friend.

I would like to think that he was waiting for me. I would like to think that he knew. I would like to think that, when I aimed that camera his way on that magic autumn day, he knew I was recording him for all of history.

His aged nobility and the incredible beauty of a proud life still glows in his eyes every time I view those photographs. Thank you, T. V. Commercial.

I would like to acknowledge the following for their help with this project: My family, for allowing me to chase horses for a living; Michael Amoruso, for his friendship and photographic expertise, for always pushing me toward my goal; Colleen Izzo, for her incredible printing talent; Wes Lanter, Tom Wade, and the Three Chimneys crew, for allowing me to bother them entirely too often; every owner and trainer who has allowed me the chance to photograph their animals, and every hotwalker and groom who has straightened a forelock for me; my sister Joan, for always inspiring me; and Guy Jenkins, for tolerating long absences, lugging my cameras around, and always offering a smile.

INTRODUCTION

oving back to Saratoga is always difficult. March, which in upstate New York still means cold, snow, and the occasional Nor'easter, is a lovely time in Florida. And, while racing has ended for the season at Gulfstream, beckoning many north, I am drawn to the incredible beauty of the opening of another Hialeah meeting.

But the Triple Crown is a waiting challenge, and the Wood Memorial calls me home. Bell South accounts are closed; NYNEX is reactivated. Banks, change of address forms, utilities companies…I can't wait to see my cats, who are still in New York with friends. The Florida landlord wouldn't allow pets.

Spring in New York can be a wonderful time. Farms are dotted with new foals, gangly characters testing new legs and snow-laced paddocks. And, as the snow grudgingly gives way, foals gain confidence and stomp their feet impatiently, challenging me and my lens. The Gotham and Wood draw me to the City, to Aqueduct and its uniquely verbal crowd. The kings of winter racing — Richard Migliore, Jorge Chavez, Gasper Moschera — still reign. Keeneland concludes and New York trainers head north for Belmont Park. I'm off to Kentucky.

The Derby is the most difficult race which I shoot. Months of anticipation are molded into Derby Day in the form of large crowds, often wet race days, and a narrow racetrack. Photographers have to sit in the dirt (or, as often, mud) along the rail, and a winner swooping five wide is impossible to see. Strike the Gold and Grindstone were both photographers' nightmares — and countless photographers will forever show negatives of Best Pal and Cavonnier as proof that those horses easily won the Run for the Roses.

The rest of the Triple Crown is something of a blur — and the hope of a sunny day at Churchill is matched only by the photographic desire for overcast days at Pimlico and Belmont Park. In between the Preakness and the Belmont, the Met Mile is nestled snuggly, still secure in its reputation as the race for future sires.

Summer is a melee of racetracks, farms, and photo labs. Laurel holds the De Francis Dash, Atlantic City hosts a wonderful day in the form of the Caesars International, and Delaware Park successfully marries the slots and the races. Belmont's racing is in full swing. Foals need identifying. Dreams swirl around cowlicks, leg positions, and negative numbers.

And it is all a waiting game — waiting for Saratoga. The race meet, while perceived by most as an endless procession of foggy mornings, is often the opposite. Some thirty days of beating the sun can be met with no reward, save exhaustion. The racing, however, is second to none. The world is in my backyard.

By the time Saratoga wraps up its season, autumn is on the wind. Paddock trees are splashed with reds and yellows, and it is a sad time as countless vans trek down to the Thruway, forking out onto New York- and Kentucky-bound routes.

Autumn is stallion conformation time. Stallion register deadlines, stallions with weight back on, cooler mornings, and a lack of flies help to make this the perfect time for one of my favorite activities. Trying to record, perfectly, an often not-too-patient model is a very time-consuming task. It is one of my favorite challenges.

While autumn can be sad, as leaves swirl about the feet rather than overhead, the knowledge that winter is ahead makes those autumn days all the more cherished. Then it's on to the Breeders' Cup, a wonderful culmination of a year of race chasing. It is a good time, a time of answers and sometimes more questions.

I cannot wait for winter now. The snow is a beautiful cover, hiding all of the plainness of late autumn. Horses in snow have an ethereal look, a magic which eludes the other seasons. And while such photographs are often miserable to take, with sub-freezing temperatures and often impressive windchill factors, the satisfaction of a beautiful image is worth the effort.

And besides, in no time, we will be back down to the sunshine and warmth of Florida. I only hope that, this time, my Florida landlord will allow cats.

It is no small thing…to have lived light in the spring.

— MATTHEW ARNOLD

Spring

New arrival, foal by Thunder Puddles out of Sligo River, Highcliff Farm, Delanson, New Yor

venty minutes old, Highcliff Farm

Bonding, Highcliff Farm

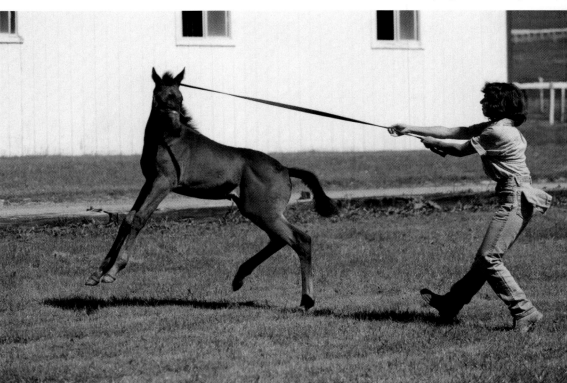

Nureyev, Walmac International, Lexington, Kentucky

Waiting to be bred, Country Life Farm, Bel Air, Maryland

Citidancer, Country Life Farm

Silver Goblin working, Dale Cordova up, Oaklawn Park

Oaklawn Park, Hot Springs, Arkansas

Trainer Larry Robideaux, Oaklawn Park

Entrance, Oaklawn Park

Statue, Keeneland

Morning gallop, Keeneland

Keeneland

Dogwoods in bloom, Keeneland

Back to the barn, Keeneland

Training track, Keeneland

Keeneland outrider

Mourning doves, Keeneland

23

Strike the Gold, Vinery, Midway, Kentucky

Mares and foals, Prestonwood Farm, Versailles, Kentucky

Silver Ghost, Vinery

Old timer, Lexington, Kentucky

Mare and foal, Keane Stud, Amenia, New York

Lead shanks, Country Life Farm

To the shed, Highcliff Farm

Claiborne Farm cemetery, Paris, Kentucky;
Secretariat's grave

SECRETARIAT
1970 — 1989

Fair Play

Fair Play statue, Normandy Farm, Lexington, Kentucky

28

Domino's grave, Mt. Brilliant Farm, Lexington, Kentucky

Man o' War's grave, Kentucky Horse Park, Lexington, Kentucky

Nick Zito's tack

Sunrise, Churchill Downs

Nighttime, Churchill Downs

Morning works, Churchill Downs, Louisville, Kentucky

Skip Away, Churchill morning gallop

Pulpit and Frank Brothers, Derby week

Derby rose

Kentucky Derby first turn, Pulpit and Free House in lead

Silver Charm, 1997 Kentucky Derby winner

Timber Country, 1995 Preakness Stakes winner

Mack Miller, Churchill Downs

Charlie Whittingham,
Pimlico Race Course, Baltimore, Maryland

Nick Zito and Pat Day, Preakness 1996

Sunday Silence and Easy Goer, 1989 Preakness Stake

38

The winning Preakness colors

122nd PREAKNESS STAKES

Starting gate, Pimlico

Bob Lewis (Beverly in background), Alibi Breakfast, Pimlico

Bob Baffert, Preakness winner's circl

Preakness wreath

Thunder Gulch after the 1995 Preakness

Wayne Lukas, casting a long shadow, Belmont Park, Elmont, New York

Wayne Lukas with Timber Country, Belmont Stakes week

Touch Gold, 1997 Belmont Stakes

Silver Charm's Belmont arriv

44

Belmont Park paddock

Jockeys to the paddock, Belmont Park

49

Belmont morning

Skeaping's Secretariat, Belmont Park paddock

Detail of a rail, Belmont Park paddock

Rokeby Stable tack, Belmont Park

Groom, Belmont Park

Gary Sciacca barn, Belmont Park

Private barn, Delaware Park, Wilmington, Delaware

Tunnel, Woodbine, Rexdale, Ontario, Cana

Atlantic City patron, Atlantic City, New Jersey

Monmouth Park, Oceanport, New Jersey

Randy Romero

Trainer Gasper Moschera with friend at Saratoga

Saratoga yearling sale

Million-dollar Devil's Bag yearling, Saratoga sales

pping for the sales, Saratoga

Fog at dawn, Oklahoma track, Saratog

Jose Santos, Saratoga

Before dawn, Saratoga

Starting gate, Saratoga

Ponying, Saratoga

Saddles, Saratoga

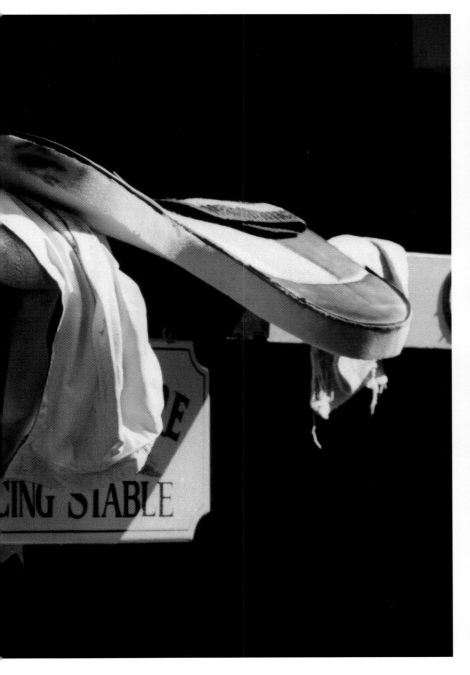

Wraps, Saratoga

Dawn at the Lukas barn, Saratoga

Hosing, Saratoga

66

Laffitte the Pirate, after the race, Saratoga

The bath, Saratoga

Turf race, Saratog

Out of the gate, Saratoga

Waiting, Saratoga

Julie Krone up, Saratoga

Fourstars Allstar, Saratoga

After the race, Saratoga

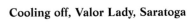

Cooling off, Valor Lady, Saratoga

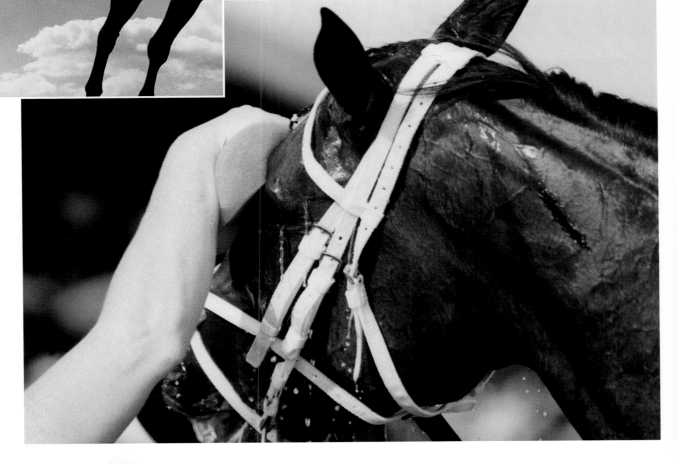

71

Final turn, Oklahoma track, Saratoga

Scotty Schulhofer, Saratoga

Oklahoma track, Saratoga

Royal Haven with owner Barbara Davis, Saratoga

Fred Hooper at age 96, Saratoga

ving out, end of Saratoga meeting

Morning after, Saratoga

Awesome Again, Saratoga stakes barn

Ivy turns, Belmont Park clubhouse

To the paddock, Belmont Park

Bookends, Belmont Park paddock

To the track, Belmont Park

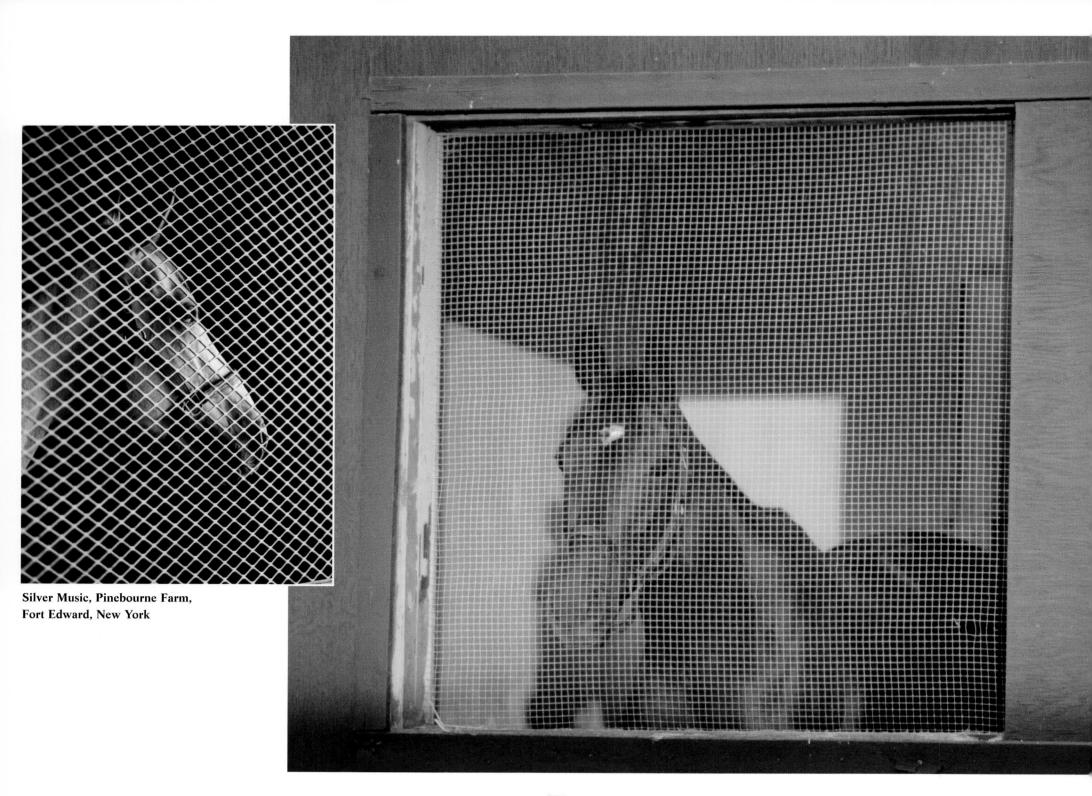

Silver Music, Pinebourne Farm,
Fort Edward, New York

Brushes

Morning light, Phipps barn, Belmont Park

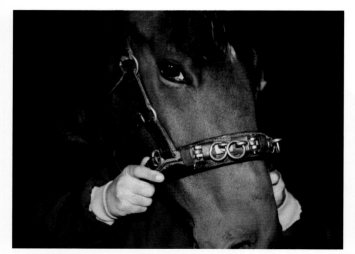

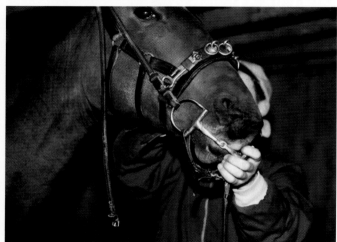

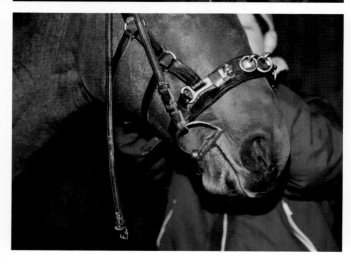

Ready to longe, Doninga Farm

In the round pen, Doninga Farm

Accepting weight

Rider up

Breaking time, Stepwise Farm, Saratoga Springs, New York

On the training track, Gainesway Farm, Lexington, Kentucky

Training yearlings, Stepwise Farm

89

Loach, The Farm at Saratoga

Young horses and the babysitter, Northview Stallion Station

Milfer Farm, Unadilla, New York

Ready to train, Oklahoma track, Saratoga

"Socks," Three Chimneys Farm

Well, Three Chimneys Farm

Seattle Slew at age 23, Three Chimneys Farm, Midway, Kentuc

Morning exercise, Seattle Slew, Three Chimneys Farm

Wild Again, Three Chimneys Farm

Gate, Keeneland

Saddling area, Keeneland

Winner's circle, benches, Keeneland

Fall foliage, Keeneland

Pond, Saratoga

Paddock, Keeneland

Riding, Keeneland

Far side, Keeneland

Morning, Keeneland

After training, Saratoga

Turkoman colt, Oklahoma track, Saratoga

Dawn on the Oklahoma track, Saratoga

Stallion bath, Northview Stallion Station

Sunrise, Northview Stallion Station

To the track, Saratoga

Working, Oklahoma track, Saratoga

Mott barn (formerly Greentree), Saratoga

Churchill Downs, Breeders' Cup time

Wayne and Jeff Lukas, Santa Anita Park,
Arcadia, California

Santa Anita sunrise

Favorite Trick with Pat Byrne, Hollywood Park,
Inglewood, California

Skip Away, Breeders' Cup week, Hollywood Park

Sunset, Hollywood Park

Before dusk, Hollywood Park

Touch Gold schooling, Hollywood Park paddo

**Jenine Sahadi schooling Elmhurst,
Hollywood Park**

**Jose Santos after Chief Bearhart's
Breeders' Cup win**

The Night is mother of the Day,
The Winter of the Spring…

— JOHN GREENLEAF WHITTIER

WINTER

Cold weather gear, Belmont Park training track

First snowfall, Oklahoma track, Saratoga

112

Winter training, Belmont Park

Bundled up, Belmont Park

Before the race, Aqueduct

Horse players, Aqueduct, Ozone Park, New York

Bettor, Aqueduct

Thawing track, Aqueduct

To the post, Aqueduct

Winter racing, Aqueduct inner track

Trying to saddle, Aqueduct

Gray day at Aqueduct

Infield Christmas tree, Aquedu

In the drizzle, Aqueduct

Icy hoofprints, Aqueduct

Frozen inner track, Aqueduct

Snowfall, Saratoga

Saratoga barns

Teaser

Julie Krone up, The Farm at Saratoga

121

Tartan Farms, Ocala, Florida
(sold for a golf course)

HORSE FARM
FOR SALE
231 ACRES
INDOOR /OUTDOOR
OWNER (518) 537 6226

New York horse farm

Starter's stand, Suffolk Downs (temporarily closed), East Boston, Massachusetts

Barn, Jefferson Downs, Kenner, Louisiana

JOCKEYS ONLY

Jockeys' quarters, Jefferson Downs (defunct track)

Bayou Blurr in shed, The Farm at Saratoga

124

Cold, mare at Questroyal Stud, Hudson, New York

Wreath

Mares, The Farm at Saratoga

Foggy morning, Brookside Farms, Versailles, Kentucky

Back to the barn, Highcliff Farm

Weanlings, The Farm at Saratoga

Pregnant mare, The Farm at Saratoga

Looking for grass, The Farm at Saratoga

Ice storm, The Farm at Sarato

Mr. Prospector at age 28, Claiborne Farm

Raja Baba at age 30, Hermitage Farm, Goshen, Kentucky

Dahlia at age 28, Brookside Farm

Bold Forbes at age 25, Kentucky Horse Park

Silver Buck at age 20, Silverleaf Farm, Ocala, Florida

133

Two-year-old training, Bonnie Heath Farm, Ocala, Florida

Outside the auction ring,
Fasig-Tipton sale, Calder Race Course,
Miami, Florida

Fasig-Tipton two-year-old sale, Calder

Cigar and Bill Mott

Enjoying his paddock, Payson Park sunrise,
Indiantown, Florida

Off to train, Payson Park

Training session, Payson Park

Morning, Gulfstream Park, Hallandale, Florida

After the last, Gulfstream Park

Stained glass, Hialeah Park, Hialeah, Florida

Relief sculpture, Hialeah Park

Groom Guy Jenkins and Skipton, Hialeah Park

139

Heat exhaustion, Flying Chevron after
the Donn Handicap, Gulfstream Park

Flying Chevron being revived, Gulfstream Park

Flamingos, Hialeah Park

Confide at Gulfstream Park

Thoroughbred racehorses have always held a special appeal for Barbara D. Livingston. She grew up about 30 miles from Saratoga Race Course and took her first photographs there in 1972. At Saratoga, her lens captured a parade of champions during that decade: Secretariat, Ruffian, Forego, Affirmed, Chris Evert, Foolish Pleasure, and Seattle Slew. Not surprisingly, Livingston was hooked on her subject matter.

In 1977, she traveled to Lexington for the first time. With her mother, she visited such famous farms as Spendthrift, where she saw Nashua, and Claiborne, home to Secretariat. Her passion for capturing the unique qualities of the Thoroughbred grew, and Livingston was determined to make photography her career. In 1984, she graduated from Syracuse University with a bachelor's degree in experimental photography. She recalls that her professors frequently criticized her for finding a way to include racing in every assignment.

After graduation, Livingston lived in Lexington for a time and worked as a free-lance photographer for *The Blood-Horse* and other racing publications. In 1986, her photo of Precisionist made the cover of *The Blood-Horse*, and Livingston was well on her way.

Today, she is widely recognized as one of the top horse racing photographers in America. In addition to *The Blood-Horse*, her work has appeared on the covers of other racing publications as well as on book covers and in advertising campaigns. In addition, her photographs have appeared in such mainstream venues as *Newsweek*, *People*, *Cigar Aficionado*, and on television's MTV, MSNBC, and "Entertainment Tonight."

Livingston has won the Eclipse Award for Outstanding Photography and twice has been runner-up in that competition. Among her other awards is winning the Kentucky Derby Museum/Nikon Photo Contest in the professional category.

Livingston has given talks on photography and she regularly contributes to racing charities in the form of photographic shoots. She lives near Saratoga Springs in upstate New York.